BANKRUPTCY PICTURE BOOK

A BRIEF INTRO TO THE LAW OF BANKRUPTCY, IN PICTURES

•WELA QUAN•

Bankruptcy Law Picture Book: A Brief Intro to the Law of Bankruptcy, in Pictures

© Wela Quan and Stephanie Ben-Ishai, 2019

Published in 2019 by

Irwin Law Inc
Suite 206, 14 Duncan Street
Toronto, ON   M5H 3G8
www.irwinlaw.com

ISBN: 978-1-55221-519-7 e-book ISBN: 978-1-55221-520-3

Cataloguing in Publication available from Library and Archives Canada

Disclaimer: Alrighty folks, you get the drill, this book isn't meant to replace your actual bankruptcy textbook or bankruptcy law class or really be used in any way to claim some sort of moral superiority over those who have not read the book (though I can't stop you!). Just make sure to not use these materials in any way that is for actual bankruptcy cases and whatnot. It's a study guide. Mmmk? Thanks!

BANKRUPTCY LAW PICTURE BOOK

BANKRUPTCY

STEP 1: <u>Becoming Bankrupt</u>

- Involuntary application for bankruptcy order
- Voluntary assignment
- Involuntary failed proposal process

STEP 2:

<u>Meeting of the creditors</u>

- Notice of meeting
- Filed proofs of claim

STEP 3:

<u>Administration of Estate</u>

- Gather and monetize property of bankrupt
- Administer claims process including determining allowances and disallowances
- Determine preferences and any fraudulent conveyances and/or transfers under value

FLOW CHART

STEP 4: Discharge of Bankrupt

- Application for discharge order
- Discharge hearing to determine if discharge is absolute, conditional, or refused

STEP 5:

Discharge of Trustee

- After the completion of the administration of the bankrupt's estate

-INSIDE-

BANKRUPTCY

Bankruptcy is the legal status for when someone is unable to repay their debts to their creditors.

Bankruptcy proceedings can involve individuals and/or corporations / entities.

1. INSOLVENCIES

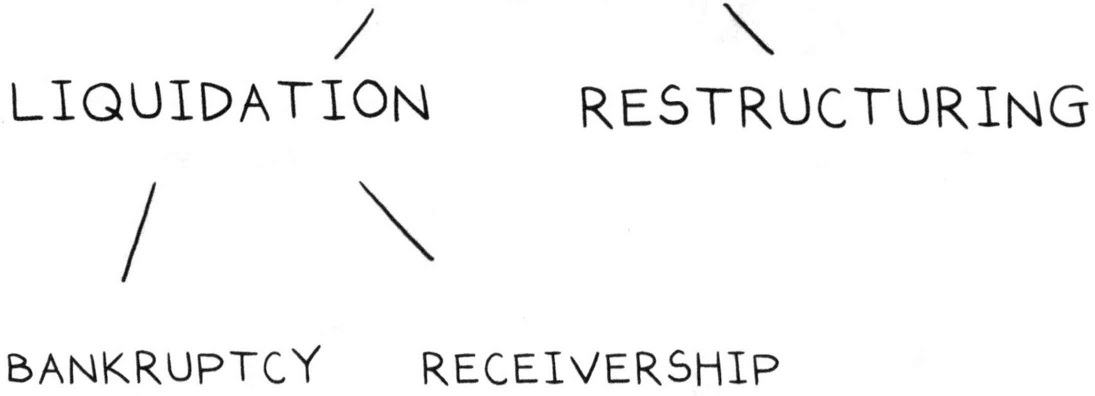

LIQUIDATION   RESTRUCTURING

BANKRUPTCY   RECEIVERSHIP

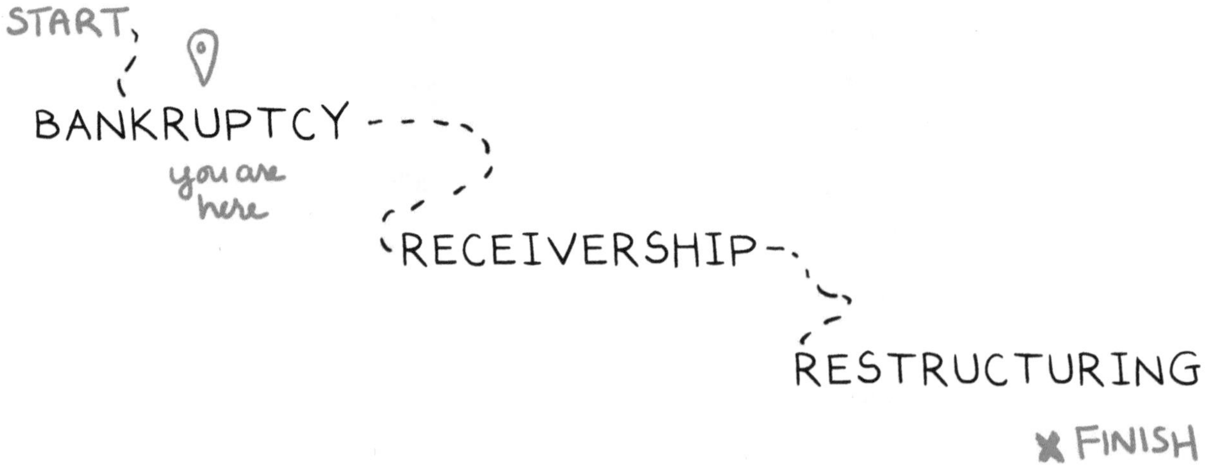

START,
BANKRUPTCY
you are here

RECEIVERSHIP

RESTRUCTURING

✖ FINISH

1. INSOLVENCIES

Insolvency is the financial state of when someone has more debt than they are able to repay.

Note that an insolvent person or entity may not necessarily be in a bankruptcy proceeding, but a bankruptcy proceeding necessarily involves insolvent people or entities.

1. INSOLVENCIES

When a person or entity becomes insolvent, there are two types of proceedings that may occur.

- Liquidations

(bankruptcies, receiverships)

Selling assets and/or business to distribute the proceeds to creditors as debt repayment

How can you sell off my magic crystals? They're all I've got!

I needed my money back so the judge said I could.

- Restructurings

Debtor retains assets but must fix the business

I'm gonna turn the business around and you'll get your $ back with lotsa interest!

1. INSOLVENCIES

Insolvency proceedings are collective and have a single proceeding model. This means that instead of all the different creditors initiating their own proceedings to recover the debt, everyone is grouped together so that it is one proceeding of all creditors against the debtor(s).

Collective proceeding

1. INSOLVENCIES

A key part of insolvency law is determining whether it falls within federal law or provincial law. If there is a conflict between the federal law and the provincial law, the doctrine of Paramountcy dictates that the federal law prevails.

1. INSOLVENCIES

Note: Bankruptcy is the legal proceeding (the state of being bankrupt), but the term "bankrupt" refers to the person or entity who is in a bankruptcy proceeding.

2. BANKRUPTCY PROCEEDINGS

(1) INVOLUNTARY
- WITHIN 6 MONTHS
- INSOLVENT PERSON
- APPLICATION PROCEDURE

(2) VOLUNTARY
APPOINTMENT OF TRUSTEE

(3) DEEMED INVOLUNTARY (FAILED PROPOSAL PROCESS)

OUTCOMES:

(4) BANKRUPTCY ORDERS
- STAY OF PROCEEDINGS
- LOSS OF ASSETS

(5) SUMMARY

(6) ANNULMENT

2. BANKRUPTCY PROCEEDINGS

There are 3 ways to start a bankruptcy proceeding, including:

1) Involuntary application for bankruptcy order

2) Voluntary assignment

3) Deemed involuntary — failed proposal process.

2. BANKRUPTCY PROCEEDINGS

(1) **Involuntary Application for Bankruptcy Order**

One or more creditors can apply for a bankruptcy order against a debtor if

   a) debts owing are **over a certain amount** ($1,000 or more as stated in the Bankruptcy and Insolvency Act);

   b) the debtor has commited an **act of bankruptcy** within the **6 months** preceding the filing and;

   c) the debtor is an **insolvent** person.

2. BANKRUPTCY PROCEEDINGS

(I) Involuntary Application for Bankruptcy Order

There is an extensive list of actions which are considered an **"act of bankruptcy,"** including but not limited to:

i) the debtor makes an assignment of their property to a trustee for the benefit of their creditors;

ii) the debtor makes a fraudulent gift;

iii) the debtor, intending to delay or defeat their creditors, departs from their dwelling or country;

iv) the debtor admits they are insolvent to the creditors, etc.

2. BANKRUPTCY PROCEEDINGS

(!) Note: **Single Creditor Petitions**

The bankruptcy regime is a collective process for the benefit of multiple creditors. It should not be used for debt collection. Generally, it is harder to use the bankruptcy regime when there is only a single creditor.

2. BANKRUPTCY PROCEEDINGS

(1) Involuntary Application for Bankruptcy Order Within Preceding 6 Months

The bankruptcy regime is a very drastic measure and the system is not meant to be used by lazy creditors for old (stale) debts, which is why one of the requirements is for the act of bankruptcy to happen within the preceding 6 months.

2. BANKRUPTCY PROCEEDINGS

(1) Involuntary Application for Bankruptcy Order

　Insolvent Person

The bankruptcy regime is only for insolvent people and entities.
Debtors cannot commit an act of bankruptcy if they are
actually able to pay the debts that the creditors demand.

2. BANKRUPTCY PROCEEDINGS

(1) Involuntary Application for Bankruptcy Order

   Bankruptcy Order — Application Procedure

In order to push a debtor into bankruptcy, the creditor must

   a) apply for a bankruptcy order with an affidavit of
       verification, and

   b) give 10 days' notice.

The debtor can then file a notice of dispute.

(!) Note that cross-examination is
    allowed on the affidavit of
    verification, but is not allowed
    on the notice of dispute.

I'm pretty sure Bob is just playing chicken with me. I'm filing this bankruptcy order anyway.

2. BANKRUPTCY PROCEEDINGS

(1) Involuntary Application for Bankruptcy Order

Bankruptcy Order — Application Procedure

- If no notice of dispute is filed, the registrar signs the bankruptcy order.
- If a notice of dispute is filed, a summary hearing before the commercial court judge is scheduled. From there, either the bankruptcy order will be issued or the application will be dismissed.

16

2. BANKRUPTCY PROCEEDINGS

(2) Voluntary Assignment

An insolvent person or entity (or if deceased, the executor, administrator, or liquidator of the succession) can voluntarily make an assignment of their property for the benefit of their creditors. The assignment must be filed with a sworn statement and include the divisible property, contact information, and amounts owed to the creditors.

2. BANKRUPTCY PROCEEDINGS

(2) Voluntary Assignment
Appointment of Trustee

If the official receiver files the assignment, a trustee in bankruptcy will be appointed to the case. The trustee's job is to be a neutral administrator who takes responsibility for the financial affairs of the bankrupt and distributes the assets to the creditors.

2. BANKRUPTCY PROCEEDINGS

(3) **Deemed Involuntary** — Failed Proposal Process

An insolvent person or entity may make a proposal to the creditors regarding how to pay off the debts owed. If the proposal is accepted, then bankruptcy proceedings may be avoided since the creditors and the debtors agree on a repayment / asset splitting plan.

2. BANKRUPTCY PROCEEDINGS

(3) Deemed Involuntary — Failed Proposal Process

If the creditors cannot agree with the proposal, the court will deem that there is an assignment in bankruptcy. This can occur when there is any of the following:

1) a termination of a stay of proceeding or a termination of the proposal filing period;

2) a negative creditor vote;

3) a negative court approval;

4) a failure to perform a proposal.

2. BANKRUPTCY PROCEEDINGS

(4) Bankruptcy Orders

Stay of Proceedings

When a bankruptcy order is granted, all proceedings against the debtor by the creditors are stayed. Secured creditors, however, can generally still continue to enforce their security unless the court orders otherwise.

2. BANKRUPTCY PROCEEDINGS

(4) Bankruptcy Orders
Loss of Assets

When a bankruptcy order is granted, the debtor loses their assets (debtor loses control of their property). Loss of assets include future assets until the debt is discharged. The assets vest in the trustee, who keeps them for the benefit of the creditors.

2. BANKRUPTCY PROCEEDINGS

(5) Summary Administration

Summary administration is for non-corporate bankrupts where (after claims of secured creditors) the entire estate is not more than $15,000 (small estates).

(!) **Note:** Under summary assignment, future property cannot be considered for the determination of realizable assets of a bankrupt.

2. BANKRUPTCY PROCEEDINGS

(6) Annulling Bankruptcy

The court has the power to annul a bankruptcy order or assignment if it finds that the order or assignment was made for an improper purpose (such as getting an unfair advantage, etc).

2. BANKRUPTCY PROCEEDINGS

Timeline of Bankruptcy Events

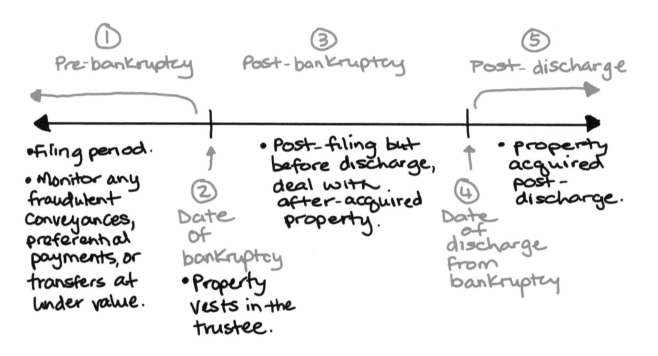

① Pre-bankruptcy

③ Post-bankruptcy

⑤ Post-discharge

• Filing period.
• Monitor any fraudulent conveyances, preferential payments, or transfers at under value.

② Date of bankruptcy
• Property vests in the trustee.

• Post-filing but before discharge, deal with after-acquired property.

④ Date of discharge from bankruptcy

• property acquired post-discharge.

3. BANKRUPTCY PROPERTY

(1) PROPERTY:
WHAT IS INCLUDED
IN BANKRUPTCIES

(2) PROPERTY:
WHAT IS EXCLUDED
FROM BANKRUPTCIES

(A) SECURED CREDITOR CLAIMS
(B) TRUSTS
    1. EXPRESS TRUSTS
    2. RESULTING TRUSTS
    3. CONSTRUCTIVE TRUSTS
(C) CERTAIN EXEMPT PROPERTY
(D) BONA FIDE PURCHASER
(E) SET-OFF
    1. LEGAL
    2. EQUITABLE
    3. CONTRACTUAL

3. BANKRUPTCY PROPERTY

(1) Property – What Is Included in Bankruptcies

The definition of property under bankruptcy law is very wide and includes every type of property located anywhere in the world, including after-acquired property.

3. BANKRUPTCY PROPERTY

(1) Property — What Is Included in Bankruptcies

The definition of property under bankruptcy law is so wide that it is even wider than the common law definition because it even includes things like licences, causes of actions, and entitlements.

3. BANKRUPTCY PROPERTY

(2) Property — What Is Excluded from Bankruptcies

Even though the definition of property is very wide, there are certain categories of property that are excluded. The following are some categories of property not available to the creditors:

- Property held by the bankrupt in trust for another person.
- Property exempt from execution by applicable provincial laws.
- Property in an RRSP (Registered Retirement Savings Plan) other than contributions in the 12 months before bankruptcy.

3. BANKRUPTCY PROPERTY

(2) Property — What Is Excluded from Bankruptcies

In sum, excluded property that is considered "out of the pot" for creditors include:

a) secured creditor claims;

b) trusts;

c) certain exempt property;

d) bona fide purchasers; and

e) set-off.

Bob. I'm trying to help you here. I've talked to Billy. There is no trust for the stones.

That's right. I have no trust for you!

3. BANKRUPTCY PROPERTY

(2) Property — What Is Excluded from Bankruptcies

(a) Secured Creditors/Claims

Secured creditors are creditors who have a charge against a debtor's property so that if the debtor fails to pay, they are allowed to seize the property itself.

Bankruptcy regime deals with the rights of **unsecured creditors**. This means that generally speaking, bankruptcy proceedings such as vesting, stays, and priorities do not affect secured creditors' claims.

Sam the Secured Creditor.

3. BANKRUPTCY PROPERTY

(2) Property — What Is Excluded from Bankruptcies

(b) Trusts

Property held in trust for others is excluded from the claims of creditors in bankruptcy. This makes sense because the property held in trust does not belong to the bankrupt. Common law principles are used to determine if a trust exists, including:

a) intention to create trust,

b) subject matter of the trust and,

c) the trust objects or purposes.

3. BANKRUPTCY PROPERTY

(2) Property – What Is Excluded from Bankruptcies

(b) Trusts

Types of trusts include:

1) Express Trusts – created by a will, agreement, or declaration;

2) Resulting Trusts (Quistclose) – these are funds provided for a specific purpose; and

3) Constructive Trusts – a trust imposed by law.

3. BANKRUPTCY PROPERTY

(2) Property — What Is Excluded from Bankruptcies

(b) Trusts

A Word on Constructive Trusts:

Constructive trusts are imposed by law to prevent unjust enrichment. A constructive trust significantly alters the priority of creditors and essentially elevates unsecured creditors to the level of secured creditors. This is why in bankruptcy the law imposes them very cautiously and uses them very rarely.

3. BANKRUPTCY PROPERTY

(2) Property — What Is Excluded from Bankruptcies

(c) Certain Exempt Property

Certain property is exempt depending on provincial law. This is
to allow bankrupts to be able to keep themselves off of social
assistance and to allow for the bankrupt to have a fresh start
after discharging their debts. Examples include things like clothing,
household furnishings up to a certain amount, tools used in the
person's trade etc.

Wait, it says here I can keep my shirt!

That makes sense. We wouldn't want people walking around literally shirtless.

3. BANKRUPTCY PROPERTY

The timeline of exempt property in bankruptcy is as follows:

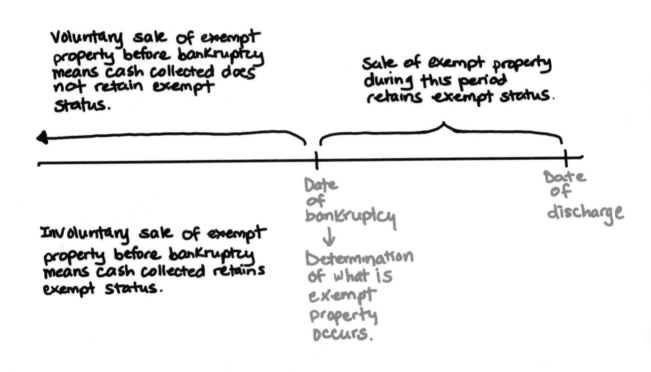

Voluntary sale of exempt property before bankruptcy means cash collected does not retain exempt status.

Sale of exempt property during this period retains exempt status.

Involuntary sale of exempt property before bankruptcy means cash collected retains exempt status.

Date of bankruptcy
↓
Determination of what is exempt property occurs.

Date of discharge

3. BANKRUPTCY PROPERTY

(2) Property — What Is Excluded from Bankruptcies

(d) Bona Fide Purchasers

Since the property of the bankrupt vests in the trustee, the bankrupt loses the right to sell the property. If the bankrupt then still sells an asset to a bona fide purchaser for value and without notice, the purchaser does not get the title to the property, but will have a post-bankruptcy claim for breach of contract, which is not discharged after bankruptcy.

Of course everything is fine! You should buy my stones!

Bona fide purchaser Bonnie, who does not know that Broke Bob is in bankruptcy and is not legally allowed to sell his property.

3. BANKRUPTCY PROPERTY

(2) Property — What Is Excluded from Bankruptcies

(e) Set-Off

Also known as "compensation," set-off allows the parties to offset mutual debts by circumventing the impact of bankruptcy. The math works in the following ways:

Example: A owes B $100,   B owes A $50
(B is the bankrupt in this example.)

Normal Bankruptcy Rules:

- A pays B's estate $100.

- A has claim in B's estate for $50 owed to A.

- Division of estate occurs and A's dividend might only be 50% → 50% of $50 is $25.

- A is out $75 instead of $50.

Set-Off:

- A owes B $100 and B owes A $50.

- Set-off means that A now simply owes B $50.

38

3. BANKRUPTCY PROPERTY

(2) Property — What Is Excluded from Bankruptcies

  (e) Set-Off — There are 3 types of set-off, including:

    1) legal,

    2) equitable, and

    3) contractual.

Legal Set-Off

- both debts must be liquidated amounts (ascertainable w/ certainty)
- both debts must be mutually owed to the same parties and w/ the same rights
- no need for there to be a transactional connection between the debts

Equitable Set-Off

- Can both be unliquidated and no need for mutuality
- there must be a close connection in the debts such that it would be inequitable to deny the right of set-off.

Contractual Set-Off
- governed by terms of the contract between the parties

3. BANKRUPTCY PROPERTY

(2) Property — What Is Excluded from Bankruptcies

(e) Set-Off

Example:

I owe you $100 but you owe me $50. But everything must go into the bankruptcy pot and your share might get reduced.

That's terrible for me.

Normal bankruptcy proceedings

I owe you $100 but you owe me $50. Here's $50.

Sounds good. I'll take the $50 and we'll call it even.

A set-off situation that avoids the complexity of bankruptcy calculations

3. BANKRUPTCY PROPERTY

The Concept of Pari Passu

In bankruptcy, pari passu means "on the same footing," or, in other words, treated equally without preference. This is a central concept that protects creditors in a bankruptcy so that creditors can divide assets without partiality and are ranked equally, as bankruptcy is a collective proceeding.

4. PRE-BANKRUPTCY TRANSFERS

(1) FRAUDULENT CONVEYANCES

(2) TRANSFERS AT UNDERVALUE

(3) PREFERENCES

4. PRE-BANKRUPTCY TRANSFERS

Going bankrupt is a very traumatic experience for individuals as well as corporations. Since all of the bankrupt's assets vest in the trustee, a bankrupt may try to transfer assets or pay certain creditors in preference to others in order to avoid having their assets divided among their creditors. This is why there are laws that stop asset transfers **before bankruptcy** to protect pari passu asset divison.

4. PRE-BANKRUPTCY TRANSFERS

Both the **BIA** and provincial laws such as **fraudulent conveyances acts** and/or **assignment and preferences acts** address unlawful transfers. Note that a fraudulent conveyance means that the asset gets transferred outside of the reach of the creditors (out of the pot), whereas a fraudulent preference means a transfer to a select creditor (for example, a friend) instead of in preference to all the general creditors.

4. PRE-BANKRUPTCY TRANSFERS

(1) Fraudulent Conveyances

When looking at whether a transfer was a fraudulent conveyance the law will consider the following:

1) Was it a **related** or arm's-length transaction?
2) Was there **consideration** or no / inadequate consideration?
3) Was the person **solvent** or insolvent at the time of transfer?
4) How long is the **look-back** / clawback period?
5) What was the **intent** of the transfer?

No, Bob. You're my brother. I love you but I am certain you're doing something fishy and I won't stand for it!

4. PRE-BANKRUPTCY TRANSFERS

(1) Fraudulent Conveyances

Some notes on the terms:

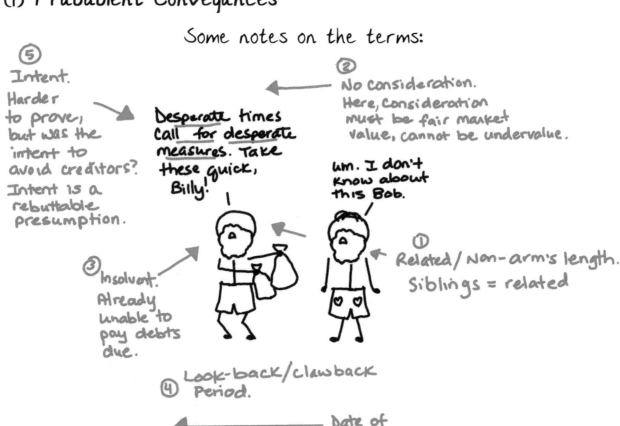

⑤ Intent. Harder to prove, but was the intent to avoid creditors? Intent is a rebuttable presumption.

② No Consideration. Here, consideration must be fair market value, cannot be undervalue.

Desperate times call for desperate measures. Take these quick, Billy!

um. I don't know about this Bob.

③ Insolvent. Already unable to pay debts due.

① Related/Non-arm's length. Siblings = related

④ Look-back/clawback Period.

Date of Bankruptcy

• Different rules for different time frames and how far back to look.
• Some improper transfers have no look-back limitation.

46

4. PRE-BANKRUPTCY TRANSFERS

(1) Fraudulent Conveyances

Under provincial law, the requirements of a fraudulent conveyance may vary. Some may not require the debtor to be insolvent, while others might not have a clawback period.

Normally, a bona fide purchaser for value is protected (i.e., the purchase is not a fraudulent conveyance).

Well, I do need some new stones for my psychic practice. I'll take some, Bob!

Bona Fide purchaser Bonnie, unaware of Broke Bob's nefarious schemes...

4. PRE-BANKRUPTCY TRANSFERS

(2) Transfers at Undervalue

Under the BIA, a transfer at undervalue is similar to fraudulent conveyances under provincial laws. Undervalue means: a disposition of property or provision of service for **no consideration** or for consideration that is conspicuously less than fair market value.

And since you're such a bon customer, you can have them at a 99% discount!

Well in that case, I'll take two!

Bon Customer Bonnie, still not suspicious?

4. PRE-BANKRUPTCY TRANSFERS

(2) Transfers at Undervalue

A transfer will be considered undervalue if the transaction was:

①
At Arm's Length

- At arm's length,
- and was made within one year,
- and the debtor was insolvent at the time,
- and the debtor intended to defeat the creditors.

↓

a transfer undervalue

Not At Arm's Length

②

- Not at arm's length,
- and was made within one year.

↓

automatically a transfer undervalue

③

- Not at arm's length,
- and was made between two to five years,
- and the debtor was insolvent at the time of the transfer,
- Or the debtor intended to defeat the creditors.

↓

a transfer undervalue

Consequences of a transfer undervalue finding include:

- transfer is found to be void and is reversed
- a monetary judgment against the debtor for the difference in consideration

4. PRE-BANKRUPTCY TRANSFERS

(3) Preferences

Under the BIA, a preference is a transfer of property or money from the debtor to a creditor on the eve of bankruptcy that is larger than the amount the creditor would have received in a bankruptcy distribution. This is unlawful because of pari passu since debtors should not prefer one creditor over another.

4. PRE-BANKRUPTCY TRANSFERS

(3) Preferences

A transfer is a preference if it is:

- a transfer of value, and
- to a creditor, and
- when the debtor was insolvent, and
- if the transfer was:

At arm's length	Not at arm's length
• 3 month look-back period	• 12-month look-back period
• look at intent of the debtor	• look at only the effect of the transfer, debtor's intent is not relevant
• debtor has rebuttable presumption	

Defences available to debtors include:

- one of the elements is not established, or
- intent was to stay in business or payment was to secured creditor.

4. PRE-BANKRUPTCY TRANSFERS

(3) Preferences

Note for corporations:

If there are reasonable grounds to believe that the corporation was insolvent when it paid a dividend or redeemed shares, a judgment against the directors for the amount of the dividend or against the shareholders for the amount of the redemption can be rendered since these corporate actions are the equivalent of gifts.

5. CONTRACTS IN BANKRUPTCY

(1) ASSET VS LIABILITY

(2) FULLY PERFORMED VS EXECUTORY (UNPERFORMED)

(3) REMEDIES FOR EXECUTORY CONTRACTS

    (A) DISCLAIMER
        1. REAL PROPERTY LEASES
        2. OTHER CONTRACTS
        3. TECHNOLOGY LICENCES
        4. SPECIFIC PERFORMANCE
    (B) AFFIRMATION
    (C) ASSIGNMENT

5. CONTRACTS IN BANKRUPTCY

Contracts form the backbone of businesses. Whether it's with employees or vendors or leases, contracts are everywhere, so when a business goes bankrupt, there are many contracts to consider. The common law remedies for breach of contract, including damages and specific performance are changed in bankrupty.

5. CONTRACTS IN BANKRUPTCY

(1) Asset vs Liability

In bankruptcy, contracts can be either an asset ("in the money") or a liability ("out of the money"). Bankruptcy laws aim to maximize the value of asset contracts and reduce the damage of liability contracts. An example of an asset vs a liability contract includes:

Asset	Liability
• Bob has a lease with GoodPlace Mall that has 5 years left. When Bob signed the lease, his rent was for $500/mo. Now rents at GoodPlace Mall are $600/mo.	• Bill has a lease with BadPlace Mall that has 5 years left. When Bill signed his lease rent was for $500/mo. Now rents at BadPlace Mall are only $300/mo.
• Bob is only paying $500/mo. due to his lease.	• Bill is still paying $500/mo due to his lease.
• The lease is an asset.	• This lease is a liability.

5. CONTRACTS IN BANKRUPTCY

(2) Fully Performed vs Executory (Unperformed)

In bankruptcy, contracts can be either **fully performed** or **executory (unperformed)**.

A fully performed contract is where one of the counterparties has done everything required under the contract.

Example: Willy supplies widgets to Bob. Bob has 30 days to pay Willy. But in the meantime

on day 13...

Scenario (A)

Bob goes bankrupt and still owes $ for the widgets

Remedy for Willy in bankruptcy:

Willy files proof that Bob owes him $ and shares, in pari passu division as an unsecured creditor.

You got the widgets Bob?

Yep. I'll pay you in 30 days.

Scenario (B)

Willy goes bankrupt before collecting payment.

Remedy for Willy's trustee in bankruptcy:

Willy's trustee sues Bob for the price of the widgets or sues for damages.

5. CONTRACTS IN BANKRUPTCY

(2) Fully Performed vs Executory (Unperformed)

An executory contract in bankruptcy is where both parties still owe ongoing obligations to each other under the contract. An example of a executory contract can be equipment leases. In bankruptcy, executory contracts can be:

1) **disclaimed,**

2) **affirmed,** or

3) **assigned.**

5. CONTRACTS IN BANKRUPTCY

(3) Remedies for Executory Contracts

 (a) Disclaimer

The remedy of disclaimer is applied slightly differently depending on the type of contract at issue. Distinctions are made between:

1) real property leases,

2) other contracts,

3) technology licences, and

4) specific performance.

5. CONTRACTS IN BANKRUPTCY

(3) Remedies

(a) Disclaimer

The remedy of disclaimer is very narrow because it is a common law power that gives the trustee the freedom not to perform the contract. (A statutory exception exists for real property leases.)

5. CONTRACTS IN BANKRUPTCY

(3) Remedies

(a) Disclaimer

Real Property Leases

Real property leases can be disclaimed. When a lease is disclaimed, the property owner has a preferred claim on: 3 months of pre-bankruptcy filing rent payment plus 3 months of post-bankruptcy accelerated rent payment. This is capped by the value of the lease and cannot be for more than 3 months of accelerated payment.

5. CONTRACTS IN BANKRUPTCY

(3) Remedies

(1) Disclaimer

Other Contracts

As stated before, except for leases, contracts cannot be disclaimed in bankruptcy. Bankruptcy also does not automatically terminate executory contracts. The trustee must elect the remedy within a reasonable amount of time to mitigate damages.

5. CONTRACTS IN BANKRUPTCY

(3) Remedies

(a) Disclaimer

Technology Licences

Where a debtor has granted a right to use intellectual property, the grantee's right is not affected by bankruptcy and may continue to use and even enforce an exclusive use right during the term of the agreement, as long as that party continues to perform its obligations under the agreement to the use of the IP.

5. CONTRACTS IN BANKRUPTCY

(3) Remedies

(l) Disclaimer

Specific Performance

Even though outside of bankruptcy a counterparty would have a specific performance claim, usually in bankruptcy one cannot claim specific performance against a trustee. The claim will have to be for damages. Note: Very remote exceptions to the rule may exist.

5. CONTRACTS IN BANKRUPTCY

Note: Ipso Facto Provisions

Ipso facto (by the very fact) provisions are ones in contracts that stipulate the automatic termination of a contract if one of the counterparties becomes bankrupt. These provisions are detrimental to bankruptcy proceedings because they avoid dealing with the bankruptcy regime. As such, there are statutory prohibitions against ipso facto provisions, though their application to contracts remains somewhat patchwork.

5. CONTRACTS IN BANKRUPTCY

(3) Remedies

(b) Affirmation

Because a trustee is not the debtor, the trustee must positively affirm executory contracts for them to benefit the estate. For **Real Property Leases**: the trustee may elect to continue the lease. For **Other Contracts**: there are no statutory provisions, but the BIA does allow the trustee to carry on the business of the bankrupt for as long as it benefits the estate.

Not to worry, Lyle. As the trustee, I'm going to continue the lease.

Phew.

(!) Note: Without a positive affirmation, the contract is assumed to be disclaimed.

5. CONTRACTS IN BANKRUPTCY

(3) Remedies

(c) Assignment

Assignment of contracts is generally allowed in bankruptcy. For **Real Property Leases**: the trustee may elect to assign the lease so long as the business is reasonably similar to the debtor's business. For **Other Contracts**: courts may make an order to assign other contracts, taking into consideration the obligations and circumstances of the debtor and the assignee.

6. CLAIMS

(1) PROVABLE

- (A) DEFINITION
  - PRESENT
  - FUTURE
  - CONTINGENT
  - UNLIQUIDATED
- (B) PROCESS
- (C) UNQUANTIFIABLE CONTINGENT
  AND/OR UNLIQUIDATED CLAIMS

(2) UNPROVABLE
(CONSEQUENCES)

(3) RULE AGAINST
DOUBLE PROOF

(4) DISCHARGE

6. CLAIMS

(1) Provable Claims

(a) Definition

A provable claim includes: present, future, contingent, and unliquidated debts. The claims are limited to pre-bankruptcy obligations (debt must arise or be incurred before the bankruptcy date).

Exceptions to this include post-filing claims for environmental clean-up costs and/or disclaimer of contracts.

I'd like to make a claim against Bob right now.

You're too late. Provable claims are for ones accrued before the bankruptcy date.

6. CLAIMS

(1) Provable Claims

(b) Process

Since the bankruptcy regime is based on pari passu division, there is a process to determine who the legitimate creditors are and whether they have a claim to the bankruptcy pot. As a first step, the trustee sends out a "Notice of First Meeting of Creditors" and a Proof of Claim form to ascertain who the creditors are and what the claims are.

So I'm sending out this Notice of meeting and we will see who shows up to make claims.

Oh boy.

6. CLAIMS

(1) Provable Claims

(b) Process

On the first pass, the trustee will review the Proof of Claim form and the attached proof of the claim. Only provable claims are part of the process. From there the trustee can:

(a) allow the claim, (b) disallow the claim, or (c) partially disallow the claim. Creditors can then appeal any disallowed or partially disallowed claims.

Now that all the proof of claim forms have come back, it's time to see if any of these are disallowed.

— Here's a hoping!

6. CLAIMS

(1) Provable Claims

(c) Unquantifiable contingent and/or unliquidated claims

Trustees will attempt to value contingent and/or unliquidated claims but some claims are too uncertain to value, which means they are not provable. Only provable claims are discharged at the end of the bankruptcy process, so unquantifiable contingent or unliquidated claims remain and are not discharged after bankruptcy.

I'm still coming after you Bob.

Unfortunately, unquantifiable debts are not discharged, you'll have to settle them post-bankruptcy.

6. CLAIMS

(2) Unprovable (Consequences)

The consequences of being unable to prove a claim are that the claimaint cannot vote and cannot receive distributions. In bankruptcy, there is no bar on the date of claims, but there are no rights to past distrbutions.

6. CLAIMS

(3) Rule Against Double Proof

Even if they are separate contracts, the bankruptcy proceeding will not allow two proofs of claim to be filed for the same debt.

6. CLAIMS

(4) Discharge

The bankruptcy process is to allow debtors to start over. The assets of the debtor are distributed and once that's done, the debts are discharged and the debtor gets a fresh start.

(!) Note: Corporate insolvencies function slightly differently and so the rules of discharge only apply to individual bankruptcies.

6. CLAIMS

In sum:

Courts must look at the facts of the cases to reach a fair conclusion. Courts generally help the weaker and more sympathetic party and are harder on parties that do not come to court with clean hands.

7. PRIORITY CREDITORS

(1) SECURED CREDITORS

(2) CROWN CLAIMS

(3) STATUTORY DEEMED TRUSTS

(4) PRIORITY FLIPS

(5) APPORTIONMENT

7. PRIORITY CREDITORS

Priority creditor classes do not participate in pari passu sharing with unsecured creditors. Priority creditors take first and unsecured creditors actually can only share in what is left. Three classes of priority creditors include:

1) **secured creditors,**
2) **crown claims,** and
3) **statutory deemed trusts.**

7. PRIORITY CREDITORS

(l) Secured Creditors

Secured creditors are not defined but are those who hold a certain type of loan that is secured by the underlying asset itself. A prime example of this is a bank that owns the mortgage on a house. Should the debtor fail to make payments on the mortgage, the bank can repossess the house. The house itself is the underlying asset that the bank can take back if the debtor defaults.

7. PRIORITY CREDITORS

(1) Secured Creditors

Secured creditors are generally unaffected by bankruptcy proceedings. All the steps of bankruptcy, including vesting of property in the trustee, distribution, and stay of proceedings, all happen subject to the rights of the secured creditors first.

7. PRIORITY CREDITORS

(1) Secured Creditors

If after a secured creditor takes its security and there is still a shortfall, the secured creditor can file a claim as an unsecured creditor for the shortfall amount. Sometimes secured creditors will leave some unsecured debt in order to be able to vote in bankruptcy proceedings.

7. PRIORITY CREDITORS

(1) Secured Creditors

Note: A secured creditor's security in the collateral must be perfected in order to take priority. Otherwise an unperfected security can lose priority to a trustee in bankruptcy. Perfection is when the security holder possesses the collateral, registers it, or gives notice that the security is collateral for a debt. (However, this rule does not apply to real property security.)

7. PRIORITY CREDITORS

(2) Crown Claims

In bankruptcy, the government gives itself priority over other private creditors using tools such as liens, charges/security interests, enhanced garnishments, and/or deemed trusts. These are social policy considerations so that public programs such as pensions and hospitals are funded first in a bankruptcy.

7. PRIORITY CREDITORS

(2) Crown Claims

Strangely enough, even though the Crown attempts to give itself priority in bankruptcy, oftentimes it does not end up being a priority creditor due to court challenges from:

a) **the federal system of government,**

b) **competing and inconsistent legislation,** and

c) **shifts in government policy.**

7. PRIORITY CREDITORS

(2) Crown Claims

Keep in mind that the doctrine of paramountcy means that federal bankruptcy laws take priority over provincial ones. But even then, there can be conflicting pieces of federal legislation and sometimes the government changes its policies completely.

7. PRIORITY CREDITORS

(3) Statutory Deemed Trusts

Examples of statutory deemed trust include: withholding taxes under the federal Income Tax Act; HST/GST under the federal Excise Tax Act; and pension contributions under provincial Pension Benefits Acts. For the most part, statutory deemed trusts are ineffective in gaining priority in bankruptcies, but withholding taxes and source deductions seem to work.

85

7. PRIORITY CREDITORS

(4) Priority Flips in Bankruptcy

Note that while outside of bankruptcy the deemed trust for HST and pension contributions take priority, in bankruptcy the secured creditor takes priority over unsecured creditors and takes priority over these statutory deemed trusts. This means that the priorities are flipped in bankruptcy and if a secured creditor takes everything and the debtor still owes HST and/or pension contributions the government gets nothing.

7. PRIORITY CREDITORS

(5) Apportionment

According to Henry VIII (from 1542), pari passu division means:

"to every of the said creditors a portion, rate and rate like, according to the quantity of their debt."

Each creditor shares in the division according to their portion.

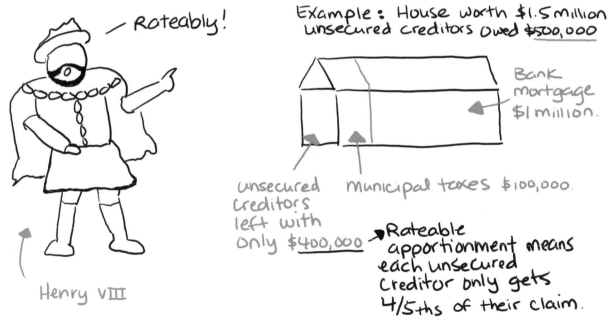

- Rateably!

Henry VIII

Example: House worth $1.5 million
unsecured creditors owed $500,000

Bank mortgage $1 million.

municipal taxes $100,000.

unsecured creditors left with only $400,000 → Rateable apportionment means each unsecured creditor only gets 4/5ths of their claim.

8. HOW TO GET PRIORITY

(1) THROUGH A
CONTRACT

(2) THROUGH A
STATUTE

ORDER OF PRIORITIES:

(A) SUPER PRIORITY STATUTORY

(B) SECURED CREDITOR CLAIMS

(C) PREFERRED CLAIMS

(D) ORDINARY UNSECURED CLAIMS

   1) UNPAID SUPPLIERS

   2) WAGE CLAIMS

   3) PENSION PLAN CLAIMS

(E) ENVIRONMENTAL CLAIMS

(F) POSTPONED CLAIMS / EQUITABLE SUBORDINATION

8. HOW TO GET PRIORITY

How to get priority

Priority is most commonly obtained through

(1) contracts or (2) statutes.

Debtor grants creditor security.

Examples include:
- mortgages
- general security agreements
- secured debentures
- notes.

Statute deems certain securities have priority

Examples include:
- employee source deductions
- sales taxes
- pension contributions

Note: Normally the security needs to be properly registered in order to be effective against 3rd parties.

In this case, I am King!

8. HOW TO GET PRIORITY

Order of Priority

The order of priority in bankruptcy is normally as follows:

a) **superpriority statutory claims** such as source deductions,

b) **secured creditors** in relative priority to their publication,

c) **preferred claims,**

d) **ordinary unsecured claims,**

e) **environmental claims,**

f) **postponed claims /** equitable subordination.

Well that's a long list of creditors.

Yeah. Yeah it is.

8. HOW TO GET PRIORITY

(c) Preferred Claims

We have already discussed statutory claims as well as secured claims (which are not really part of the bankruptcy proceeding in the first place). We now come to preferred claims. **Preferred claims** are a subset of unsecured claims. They include: funeral expenses, cost of administration, superintendent's levy, certain wage arrears, unsecured municipal taxes, certain arrears/accelerated rent to property owners, and others.

8. HOW TO GET PRIORITY

(d) Unsecured Claims — Special Cases

There are several special cases within the category of unsecured creditors, including:

1) **unpaid suppliers,**
2) **wage claims,** and
3) **pension fund claims.**

How many special exceptions are there?

A lot. Yeah, the law is not so tidy.

8. HOW TO GET PRIORITY

(d) Unsecured

1. Unpaid Suppliers

An unpaid supplier may have the right to repossess goods as long as the transaction meets a very specific laundry list of criteria that includes but is not limited to the following:

- Supplier presents written demand,
- in prescribed form,
- within 15 days after the day on which the purchaser became bankrupt,
- the goods were delivered within 30 days before the day on which the purchaser became bankrupt,
- at the time of the demand the goods are in the possession of the purchaser or trustee, etc.

I mean this really is ineffective to help suppliers because there are many rules.

8. HOW TO GET PRIORITY

(d) Unsecured

2. Wage Claims

When a business goes bankrupt, it can be devastating for its employees. For public policy reasons, the government has granted employees a limited superpriority to protect them when it comes to wage arrears. There is a 6 month look-back period and a cap of $2,000. "Wage" includes salaries, commissions, and vacation pay, but does not include termination or severance pay.

8. HOW TO GET PRIORITY

(d) Unsecured

3. Pension Fund Claims

As with wage claims, the government has granted a limited superpriority to protect pension fund claims. As with wage claims, pensioners (former employees) become involuntary creditors. But unlike wage claims, the superpriority gives a security over all assets (not just current assets like in wage claims) and there is no cap on the claims.

8. HOW TO GET PRIORITY

(e) Environmental Claims

A super–lien is attached to real property for any amounts spent by the Crown for remedying any environmental conditions affecting the real property. Clean–up costs do not have any special priority, but the trustee is afforded special protections against liability that might arise from environmental claims.

8. HOW TO GET PRIORITY

(f) Postponed Claims / Equitable Subordination

Last but not least, there are postponed claims of non-arm's length creditors, silent partners, and preferred wage claims of officers or directors. In some cases inequitable conduct may be found; the remedy in the United States is to subordinate the wrongdoer's claims, and in Canada the oppression remedy is a possibility.

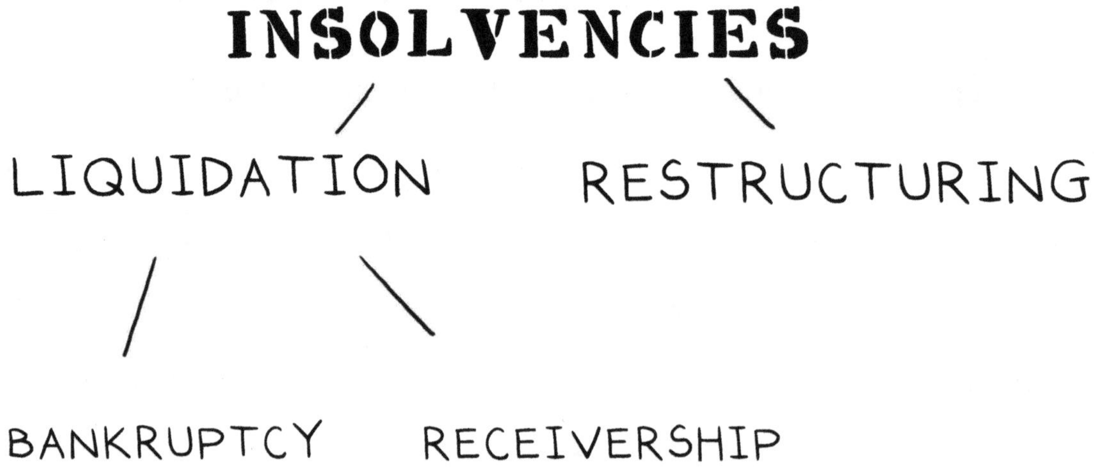

INSOLVENCIES

LIQUIDATION   RESTRUCTURING

BANKRUPTCY   RECEIVERSHIP

START,

BANKRUPTCY - - -

RECEIVERSHIP - -

you are here

RESTRUCTURING

✗ FINISH

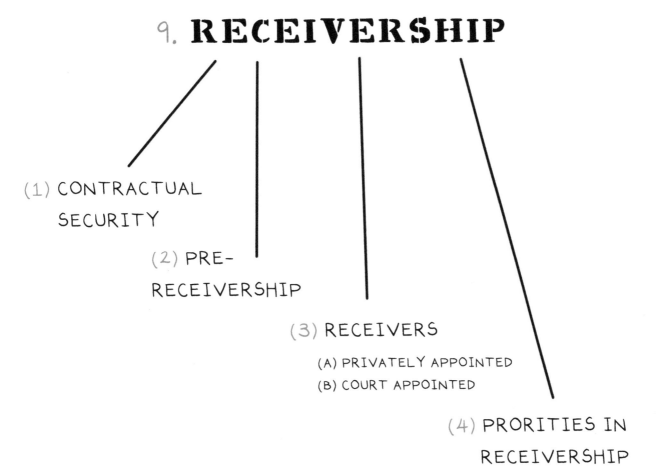

9. RECEIVERSHIP

(1) CONTRACTUAL SECURITY

(2) PRE-RECEIVERSHIP

(3) RECEIVERS

    (A) PRIVATELY APPOINTED

    (B) COURT APPOINTED

(4) PRORITIES IN RECEIVERSHIP

9. RECEIVERSHIP

There are two major liquidation regimes.

The first one is bankruptcy, which has been covered.

The second one is receivership.

Receivership proceedings are when a secured creditor seeks to recover money that they have lent to the borrower by selling a debtor's business or assets (collateral), or if a court appoints one to intervene in acrimonious liquidation situations.

9. RECEIVERSHIP

(1) Contractual Security

Normally, if a bank lends money, they will take security in the borrower's assets (collateral) as insurance if the borrower defaults. This is a contractual security. If a borrower defaults, the bank's receiver can take possession of the collateral and sell it as repayment of the loans. Typically, professional accounting firms act as receivers.

9. RECEIVERSHIP

(1) Contractual Security

There are different types of contractual security including:

Simple

Ex: mortgage on house

Remedies for default:

- possession
- foreclosure
- seizure and sale
- sue for monetary judgment

Sophisticated

Ex: general security agreement (GSA), secured notes, secured debentures

Remedies for default:

- possession
- foreclosure
- seizure and sale
- receivership

A GSA grants lenders security over all categories of a business's assets and provides lenders with a range of remedies on default, including powers to appoint a receiver and/or even operate the business pending sale / liquidation.

9. RECEIVERSHIP

(2) Pre-receivership

Pre-receivership steps and requirements

Step 1: Review the security agreement to check for <u>default</u> and /or <u>receivership provisions</u> in the agreement.

Step 2: Review the contractual <u>"events of default."</u>
　　　↳ Consider contractual notice and <u>cure periods.</u>
　　　↳ Consider if the loan is a <u>"demand loan."</u>
　　　　　　　　　　　　　　　↓

　　　　　　　　　　　　If <u>yes</u>, consider the <u>demand period.</u>

Step 3: Before enforcing the security, consider if it's possible to enter into a <u>"forbearance agreement."</u>

Step 4: If nothing can be done, the final step is to give <u>"notice of intent to enforce security."</u>

9. RECEIVERSHIP

A secured creditor who intends to enforce a security on substantially all of the debtor's inventory used in a business must send a **Notice of Intent to Enforce Security.**

The secured creditor cannot enforce until 10 days after sending the notice (unless the insolvent person consents to allow the enforcement earlier).

9. RECEIVERSHIP

(3) Receivers

Basis to appoint a Receiver and Receiver Types

Basis

- Contractual right to appoint a receiver
- Equitable appointment
- Other statutory provisions

Types

- Receiver manager
- Privately appointed under security agreements
- Court appointed
- Interim receivers

Only a licenced trustee may act as a receiver.

9. RECEIVERSHIP

(3) Receivers

(a) Privately Appointed Receivers

Privately appointed receivers used to be quite common and simple because they could be appointed by a simple letter from the creditor with no court involvement. They are now rarely used because without the court involved, lenders are exposed to liability, having to be responsible for their appointed receivers. Private receivers also cannot "breach the peace," which means that if the debtor does not cooperate the receiver cannot take possession of the assets.

And what happens if I don't give you my stuff?

Well since I'm not a private receiver I'm allowed to ask my friend here to, uh..."disturb your peace"...

9. RECEIVERSHIP

(3) Receivers

(b) Court-Appointed Receivers

Court-appointed receivers are granted the power to take possession of all the insolvent person's assets and/or their business in order to exercise control or take any other actions the court deems advisable. In the court order to appoint a receiver, the receiver's powers are set out in detail, as is the access to assets, the receiver's limitation of liability, the funding of the receivership, and other information.

The court order gives me the power to take your stuff.

9. RECEIVERSHIP

(3) Receivers

(b) Court-Appointed Receivers — Role

Court-appointed receivers are not agents of the lender but instead are officers of the court. They have largely replaced private receivers and are considered part of an equitable remedy under the court's discretion. The receiver relies on the protection of the court and the court order creates a first charge on all assets controlled by the receiver to secure the receiver's costs.

Why should I trust you with my stuff, you're the creditor's crony.

That's just not true. I'm court appointed. I'm no one's crony. I do what the court tells me to.

9. RECEIVERSHIP

(3) Receivers

  (b) Court-Appointed Receivers — Process

Step 1: Notice of Intent to Enforce Security
    —send to debtor, 10-days' notice period

Step 2: Filing of Application to Commercial Court for appointment of receiver
    - debtor can file responding material, cross-examine on affidavits, and/or object to appointment
    - court then issues an appointment order

Step 3: Receiver takes Control / Secures Assets
    - receiver at this point is either operating the business or has taken control of the assets
    - decision is made on sale/liquidation
    - court issues sale approval order

Step 4: Distribution order
    - Court gives opinion on how the security should be distributed

Step 5: Discharge order
    - court gives an order to discharge the debt

9. RECEIVERSHIP

(4) Priorities in Receivership

1) Environmental charges

2) 30-day goods

3) Agricultural supplier charges – inventory

4) Deemed trusts for source deductions

5) Employee wage charges – $2,000

6) Pension charges

7) The rest

I owe a lot of environmental charges.

Yeah, your creditors can't do nothing about that.

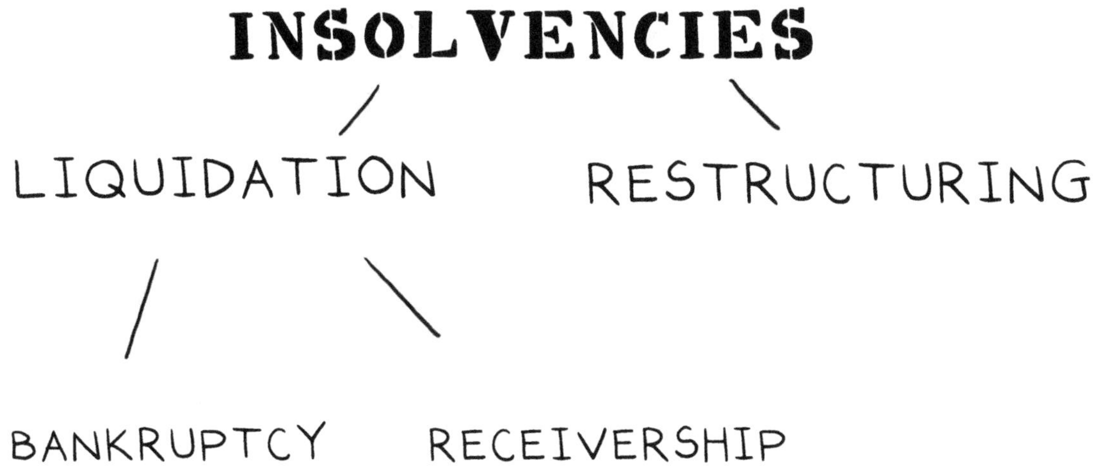

INSOLVENCIES

LIQUIDATION   RESTRUCTURING

BANKRUPTCY   RECEIVERSHIP

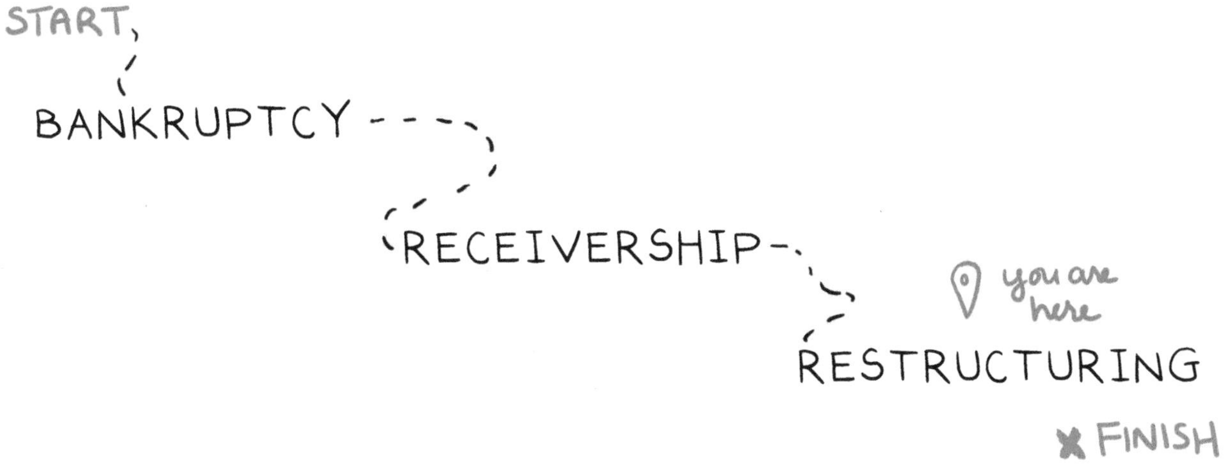

START,
  BANKRUPTCY ----
            RECEIVERSHIP---
                              ⊙ you are
                                 here
                    RESTRUCTURING
                         ✖ FINISH

10. **RESTRUCTURING**

(1) REQUIREMENTS
AND PROCESSES

(2) KEY FIGURES IN
RESTRUCTURING

(A) DIRECTORS AND THEIR
DUTIES AND LIABILITIES
1) FIDUCIARY, DUTY OF CARE
2) OPPRESSION, MISREPRESENTATION
3) STATUTORY

(B) MONITORS

(3) BUSINESS OPERATIONS
DURING RESTRUCTURING

(4) CCAA CLAIMS

(5) BIA PROPOSALS

10. RESTRUCTURING

(1) Requirements and Processes

Regimes

We have completed liquidation regimes including bankruptcy and receivership. Now we turn our attention to restructuring regimes under the Companies' Creditors Arrangement Act (CCAA) and the BIA through proposals. Differences between bankruptcy and restructuring include:

BANKRUPTCY	RESTRUCTURING
• assets vest in trustee	• debtor remains in control of the assets / business
• assets are liquidated	• stay of creditor's rights to allow for negotiation
• proceeds are distributed based on legal priorities and pari passu among unsecured creditors	• special powers are granted to vary certain rights of parties to assist in the restructure
	• restructure agreement / plan with creditors
	• court supervised, overseen by a Monitor

10. RESTRUCTURING

(1) Requirements and Processes

Objectives

There are several different objectives of restructuring; the most important one is minimizing economic hardship to employees and society at large when a company fails. Other objectives include: preserving the value of the business, helping the debtor make changes to the business so that the debtor may continue to run the business, and increasing creditor returns.

10. RESTRUCTURING

(1) Requirements and Processes

Requirements

In order to obtain creditor protection under the CCAA, the company must meet the following list of requirements:

- Canadian corporation/company incorporated in Canada or a foreign corporation with assets in Canada
  - Excluded are banks and insurance companies, limited partnerships

- Company needs to be a debtor corporation, meaning bankrupt or insolvent, have committed an act of bankruptcy, have authorized an assignment, or be in the course of being wound up

- Has a debt of more than $5 million

10. RESTRUCTURING

(1) Requirements and Processes

Initial Order

In the initial restructuring order, the following things are set out:

- Possession of the business operations and property
- Appointment of a monitor and the monitor's powers
- Stays of proceedings and rights
- Protection of directors and officers
- Debtor in possession financing
- Restructuring powers
- Priority of the charges
- Other general provisions

10. RESTRUCTURING

(1) Requirements and Processes

Initial Application

After the filing of the initial application, the stay of proceedings is normally for 30 days and only the court can extend that time. Normally one judge is appointed for the proceeding.

10. RESTRUCTURING

(1) Requirements and Processes

"Debtor in Possession"

In a restructuring, the debtor remains in possession and control of its asset and/or business. This is what is meant by the term "debtor in possession."

Bankruptcy	Receivership	Restructuring
• Debtor's assets vest in the trustee	• Debtor's assets are controlled and possessed by the receiver	• Debtor's assets remain in the control and possession of the debtor.

(!) Note: The pre-restructuring board of directors remains in control and supervision of the process is carried out by the monitor and the court.

10. RESTRUCTURING

(1) Requirements and Processes
Governance During Restructuring

Governance of a company during restructuring is not significantly different from ordinary governance of the company. Normally a company has a **Board of Directors** and **Management.**

<u>Board of Directors</u>

- selects and oversees management

- duty to supervise the affairs of the business

- information about the business is limited as it is provided by management
- meets several times a year

<u>Management</u>

- people who actually operate the business such as the CEO, CFO, COO, etc.

- full access to company's info

- full-time / hands-on job

Note: During a restructuring, it is possible for the board of directors and the management to have a conflict of interest. Example: if the board wants to layoff employees, whereas management wants to keep those jobs.

10. RESTRUCTURING

(2) Key Figures in Restructuring

(a) Directors and their duties and liabilities

Directors and officers owe a **Fiduciary Duty** to the company and must act with a **Duty of Care.**

Fiduciary Duty	Duty of Care
• to act in good faith to the best interests of the Company	• exercise care, diligence, skill that a reasonably prudent person would exercise
• avoid conflicts of interest	• Owed to all stakeholders including creditors
• not abuse the position for personal benefit	• subject to business judgment rule
• maintain confidentiality	• measured by objective test.
• serve the company honestly and selflessly	

10. RESTRUCTURING

(2) Key Figures in Restructuring

(a) Directors and their duties and liabilities

As a general rule, directors are not responsible for the liabilities of the companies they direct. There are, however, exceptions to this rule where they may attract personal liability including in **oppression** claims or **misrepresentation** claims.

Oppression	Misrepresentation
• Creditors can be complainants against the Company's directors	• a misrepresentation made by a director to a creditor regarding financial state of the company in order to get more credit.
• it is a very broad claim, no need for bad faith, illegality, or intent to injure	• this is an independent tort and attracts personal liability of the director.
• remedy is also very broad	

(2) Key Figures

(a) Directors and their duties and liabilities: Statutory

Another exception to the general rule of no director liability includes personal liability imposed by **statutes** for policy reasons in order to discourage bad behaviour, including the following:

• unpaid wages and vacation pay

• employee source deductions and employer premiums

• sales taxes

Well ms. Monitor, I don't know who the directors of this company are but they owe us a lot of unpaid wages!

10. RESTRUCTURING

(2) Key Figures

(a) Directors and their duties and liabilities: Statutory

When a company is facing financial difficulties it may fail to pay **wages** and **vacation pay.** For policy reasons, this is discouraged and directors are made responsible for a portion of these liabilities. Under the Canada Business Corporations Act, directors do have a "due diligence defence" where directors are not liable if they acted reasonably and relied in good faith on audited financial statements or a report of a professional.

10. RESTRUCTURING

(2) Key Figures

(a) Directors and their duties and liabilities: Statutory

Under statutory provisions, directors are also jointly and severally liable for unpaid **employee source deductions** (corporations are required to withhold them on account of the employee's income tax), **employer premiums,** and unpaid **sales tax.** These liabilities are both subject to certain preconditions and a due diligence defence.

I have to warn you, though — the company has to still withhold and pay taxes, so you're not going to get back as much as you think.

Argh. Tax man always wins.

10. RESTRUCTURING

Protection of Directors and Officers:
Pre-filing and Post-filing

We have seen that directors and officers do expose themselves to some liabilities in fulfilling their roles. This is why there are certain protections for them pre-/post-bankruptcy filing including:

Pre-filing Protections

- Corporate indemnities
  - → not as helpful during insolvency since it's an unsecured claim
  - → there may also be limitations in the corporate legislation on indemnification eg: not bad faith

- Directors and officers insurance
  - → this is the best form of protection

Post-filing Protections

- CCAA provides various protections for directors and officers, including
  - → stays of proceedings that arose before the commencement of proceedings
  - → charge to secure corporate indemnity subject to D&O insurance
  - → plan can contain broad release of D&O (with limitations for contractual obligations or fraud etc.)

- Date for barring claims

10. RESTRUCTURING

Director and Officers — Final Points

- On the application of any interested person in the matter, the court may make an order to remove any director of a debtor company.

- In a bankruptcy, the management of the company may be the cause of the problem or not be aligned with the directors. Good managers may also want to leave. Because of this, companies should have plans in place, especially key employee retention plans.

10. RESTRUCTURING

(2) Key Figures

(b) Monitors

Monitors are officers of the court and they are a mandatory part of restructurings. Monitors have a mandate to monitor the proceedings of the business and report this to the court and creditors, as well as assisting the debtor in the development of a restructuring plan.

You must be one of the directors. I'm Molly the Monitor. I'm here to help you develop a restructuring plan.

That plan better include paying us our wages back!

(!) Note: Monitors must be licensed trustees and are normally firms such as E&Y, KPMG, etc.

10. RESTRUCTURING

(2) Key Figures

(b) Monitors: Duties and Functions

Aside from the duty to monitor the debtor's business and report on the affairs of the business from time to time, there are certain steps in the CCAA process that specifically require reporting by the monitor, including but not limited to approval of interim financing, assignment and/or disclaimer of agreements, and interim asset sales.

10. RESTRUCTURING

(2) Key Figures

(b) Monitors: Protections for Monitors

Since monitors are court officers injected into contentious restructuring proceedings, they are exposed to claims being asserted against them. As such, they are given protection with respect to certain successor employer and environmental claims, such as: first ranking administration charges for fees, no liability except for willful misconduct or gross negligence, injunctions against proceedings against them, etc.

10. RESTRUCTURING

Other Possible Characters in a Restructuring

Chief Restructuring Officer

- stakeholders may not trust debtor company's management during restructuring
- recent practice to appoint a CRO to replace or supplement management
- role is an officer of the court, appointment can be debtor or creditor driven

Super Monitor

- sometimes a debtor company's board may resign, leaving the debtor without governance
- super monitors are monitors who are given additional powers to perform board functions

Property Owners

- can be major stakeholder in restructurings
- issues such as forced lease assignments and disclaimer of leases can be major problems in restructuring

Governments

- can be involved in various issues such as environment, pension, municipal tax, etc
- also a social stakeholder

10. RESTRUCTURING

(3) Business Operations During Restructuring

Since in a restructuring the board remains in control, several elements are required to ensure that the business can continue to operate somewhat normally. These include ensuring that there is a **stay of proceedings, debtor-in-possession (DIP) financing,** and restructuring powers to deal with **company contracts.**

Look here. I'm the monitor assigned to this company. I'm here to help ensure the business is ok during restructuring whether you like it or not. So lets just get along. ok?

10. RESTRUCTURING

(3) Business Operations — Stay of Proceedings

Courts grant a stay of proceedings in restructurings to maintain the status quo and allow the business to operate normally. There are a limited number of exceptions to this rule, including but not limited to immediate payment for goods, certain regulatory bodies, third party demands, etc.

10. RESTRUCTURING

(3) Business Operations — Interim (DIP) Financing

During restructuring, one way to keep the business running is through interim debtor-in-possession (DIP) financing. The debtor may apply to the court for an order to allow for DIP financing and the court will consider many factors in determining whether to allow the DIP financing. A monitor's recommendation is important and the DIP financing creditor ranks second to admin charges.

Also, you are not going to sell the company's assets. We'll apply for an order to get DIP financing.

Oh, I've never heard of that.

10. **RESTRUCTURING**

(3) Business Operations — Executory Contracts

  (a) Affirmations and Assignments

- **Executory Contracts and Affirmation:** Not applicable because in a restructuring the business is continuing, so all the contracts are on-going and active.

- **Executory Contracts and Assignments:** On application from the debtor, the court may make assignment of contracts. The court will consider whether the monitor approved the proposed assignment as well as whether the assignment would be appropriate.

I'm Molly the monitor and I approve of this assignment.

What is this, a campaign ad or something?

10. RESTRUCTURING

(3) Business Operations — Executory Contracts

(b) Disclaimers and Critical Suppliers

- **Executory Contracts and Disclaimers:** Debtors may disclaim agreements; however, any party to the agreement may apply to court for an order stating the agreement is not to be disclaimed. Certain exclusions apply, like collective agreements, financial agreements, etc.

- **Executory Contracts and Critical Suppliers:** Debtors may apply to the court to have a certain creditor be declared a critical supplier. The court may order that security or change rank in priority over the claim of any secured creditor of the company.

Can we disclaim this contract?

Yes, but the counterparty might disagree.

10. RESTRUCTURING

(3) Business Operations — KERPs / Collective Agreeements

Key Employee Retention Plans (KERPs) are a tool to incentivize key employees to remain in their positions during the restructuring. Unsecured creditors dislike KERPs because they see this as paying a bonus to executives.

Collective Agreements are contracts between the company and its unions. These agreements cannot be disclaimed in Canada but can be rejected in Chapter 11 bankruptcies in the United States.

10. RESTRUCTURING

(3) Business Operations — Asset Sales

A debtor company may not dispose of assets outside the ordinary course of business unless authorized to do so by a court during the restructuring. A typical process involves obtaining approval for a marketing campaign so that assets are exposed to the market. Offers are required by a set date and successful bids require court approval. A purchaser gets a vesting order which vests the asset in the purchaser free of any charges and restrictions.

10. RESTRUCTURING

(3) Business Operations – Plan of Arrangement

- The goal of the restructuring is to have the creditors and debtors agree on a plan. The plan is a statutorily mandated contract that is binding on the debtor, creditors, and even non-consenting minority creditors. Like a normal contract, it is generally only limited by the creativity of the drafters.

- The debt can be restructured in any number of creative ways, such as exchanging debt for shares of the new company, payment of percentage of the debt, etc.

- Other common elements include exit financing, appointment of new board, disposition of assets/business lines, releases, new equity, etc.

 That director was seriously clueless. No wonder the company needs a reorg.

10. RESTRUCTURING

(4) CCAA Claims

A claim under the CCAA is any indebtedness, liability, or obligation that would be **provable**. Given the nature of reorganizations, the claim has to be **able to be dealt with by a compromise or arrangement**. The **amount** of the claim must also be identified. Any disputed claim amounts are subject to a determination made by the court on a summary application.

10. RESTRUCTURING

(4) CCAA Claims — Procedure Order

In order to file a claim, the claims procedure requires that there be notification sent to known creditors and that there be advertisements to determine unknown creditors, a form of the proof of claim that must be submitted, as well as a claims bar date. There will then be a process to allow, disallow, or partially allow a claim, as well as a process for adjudication of disputed claims.

We should take out an ad so we can find any unknown creditors.

Yes. Let's see who comes out of the woodwork.

10. RESTRUCTURING

(4) CCAA Claims — Priorities

Unlike in bankruptcy, where the priorities cascade down like a waterfall, in a reorganization, the plan of arrangement determines the priority of distribution based on common law and the CCAA. Unless the priority is varied by the CCAA (e.g., statutory deemed trusts), the plan must respect the priority ranking.

10. RESTRUCTURING

(4) CCAA Claims — Creditors

Creditors in a restructuring include secured creditors, unsecured creditors, subordinated claims, Crown claims, statutory deemed trusts, 30-day goods, environmental claims, and wage and pension claims.

Secured Creditors

In restructurings, they do not get an automatic subordination of unperfected security interests like in a bankruptcy.

10. RESTRUCTURING

(4) CCAA Claims — Claims

Subordinated Claims

For the most part, courts usually respect contractual subordination or postponement.

Crown Claims

Usually unsecured, except for withholding taxes and other registered legislative security.

Statutory Deemed Trusts

Property of a debtor company is not regarded as being held in trust for the crown unless it would be regarded as such in the absence of that statutory provision.

An exception to this rule is withholding taxes.

10. RESTRUCTURING

(4) CCAA Claims — Claims

30-Day Goods

Not applicable in CCAA restructuring proceedings. The order for seizure of 30-day goods can be made, but is practically ineffective.

Environmental Claims

Secured by a charge on real property, and the monitor may choose to comply with remediation.

Wage and Pension Claims

Wage protection is not applicable in restructuring, but a court cannot sanction a restructuring plan unless employees receive at least what they would under the BIA, and pension contributions are paid in full. Courts are also prohibited from authorizing an interim sale unless pension contribution and employee claims are already paid out.

10. RESTRUCTURING

(4) CCAA Claims — Voting and Classification of Claims

In order to determine what class a creditor belongs to, courts will look at whether the creditor's rights are sufficiently similar to give them a commonality of interest. Factors to help make this determination include: the nature of debts, rank of security, remedies available to the creditor in the absence of an arrangement, and other criteria.

Wait a second. How are we so sure he belongs to the right class of creditors? I think we need to check again.

10. RESTRUCTURING

(4) CCAA Claims — Voting and Classification of Claims

The debtor company must obtain court approval of the classes before a meeting can be held. The simplest classification is to have one class of secured creditors and another class of unsecured creditors. Voting creditors need 50 percent plus one and 2/3 of the value of claims.

I'm not sure that the math works. 50% + 1 and 2/3 of the claim...

Means that, for example, 10 creditors with total claims of $100,000 need 6 creditors with voting claims totalling at least $66,666...

10. RESTRUCTURING

(4) CCAA Claims – Meeting Order

The creditors have a physical meeting (though the creditors can provide proxies to the monitor). The creditors have with them the proposed plan of arrangement as well as a report with the monitor's recommendations. The plan has to be better for the creditors than bankruptcy, and the plan then gets put to a vote.

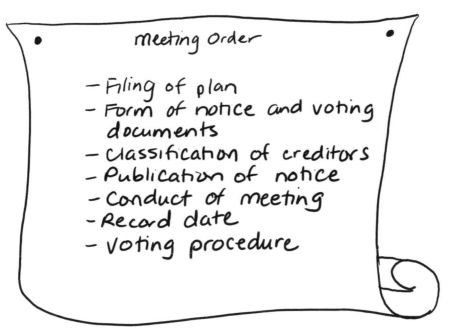

Meeting Order

- Filing of plan
- Form of notice and voting documents
- Classification of creditors
- Publication of notice
- Conduct of meeting
- Record date
- Voting procedure

10. RESTRUCTURING

(4) CCAA Claims — Other Creditors

- Acquisition of Claims: When a claim is bought at a discount by a hedge fund for profit, the purchased claims are treated as a single creditor for voting purposes.
- Equity shareholders are also considered another class. They can object to the plan at the sanction stage but usually are not allowed to vote unless permitted by the court.

(!) Note: The court cannot sanction a plan that provides for any equity claim payments unless all unsecured creditors are paid in full.

10. RESTRUCTURING

(4) CCAA Claims — Court Approval of Plans

A court cannot approve a plan without provisions for paying out source deductions, employee treatment, and pension treatment. Aside from these mandatory requirements, the court can only approve a plan that is **fair and reasonable.** The definition of fair and reasonable is broad and could include things such as third-party releases. If the plan is not approved by the creditors or sanctioned by the court, bankruptcy is likely but not automatic.

10. RESTRUCTURING

Restructuring Proceeding Summary

① Pre-planning — Arrange Proposed Monitor, Counsel

② Application for Initial Order
   - notice of application & supporting affidavits
   - draft initial order
   - sometimes monitor may prepare pre-filing report

③ Initial Order Issued
   - stay of proceedings
   - restructuring powers
   - DIP interim financing
   - appointment of monitor
   - administration charge
   - director's charge

④ Sales / Investment Solicitation Process

⑤ Interim Sale Order

⑥ Motions Regarding Contracts
   (Assignment / Disclaimers)

⑦ Distribution of Proceeds and
   Bankruptcy <u>OR</u> ... ⟶

10. RESTRUCTURING

Restructuring Proceeding Summary

⑦ Proceed to Plan of Arrangement

↓

⑧ Claims Order

↓

⑨ Meeting Order ⇢ ⑩ Meeting of creditors

↓

Shareholders, creditors, and/or the court can still reject the plan at the sanction hearing, which could lead to bankruptcy or trying to negotiate a new plan. ⟵ ⑪ Sanction Hearing

↓

⑫ Plan Implementation

• Company is restructured and will be operated according to the new plan.

10. RESTRUCTURING

(5) BIA Proposals

The BIA proposal is similar to a CCAA restructuring but is for non-consumers (applies to corporations and individuals) to restructure under court protection. This allows smaller enterprises and individuals to restructure in a less complicated, less time consuming, less costly, and less court-involved manner than under the CCAA restructuring proceeding.

CCAA Restructuring	BIA Proposal
• The more involved process to give companies a way to continue to survive without going through bankruptcy.	• A smaller-scale version of the CCAA restructuring proceeding that is less costly for smaller enterprises and individuals.

10. RESTRUCTURING

(5) BIA Proposal – Process Overview

- Step 1: Appointment of a Proposal Trustee.

  (!) Note that since the BIA proposal is a debtor-in-possession process, no assets vest in the proposal trustee.

- Step 2: Proceedings commenced by filing a Notice of Intention to make a proposal or the actual filing of the proposal (no need to obtain an Initial Order). An automatic stay of proceedings for 30 days begins.

  (!) Note: 45-day extensions can be granted for up to 180 days, after which bankruptcy is automatic if the plan was not approved, unless flipped into a CCAA or holding proposal.

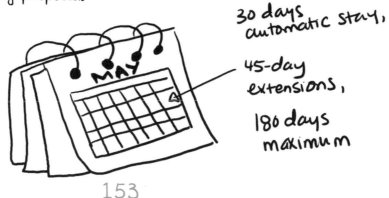

30 days automatic stay,

45-day extensions,

180 days maximum

10. RESTRUCTURING

(5) BIA Proposal — Process Overview

- Step 3: After the proposal is filed, the proposal trustee calls a meeting of the creditors and each class of unsecured creditors votes on the proposal. A negative vote among secured creditors does not mean an automatic bankruptcy, but if unsecured creditors reject the plan, then there will be an automatic bankruptcy.

- Step 4: "First Day Orders" are available for charges such as administration, directors and officers, interim financing, and critical suppliers.

Note: The proposal trustee must review the cash flow statement and it must be signed by the debtor and filed within 10 days or bankruptcy is automatic.

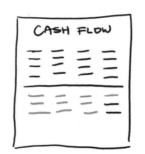
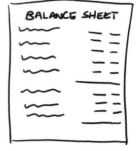

10. RESTRUCTURING

(5) BIA Proposals — Various Parties

Secured Creditors

- Secured creditors vote: if yes, then the proposal is binding on them.
- If unsecured creditors vote yes and the court approves, secured creditors are still free to exercise their rights per usual.

Preferred Creditors

- Proposal must specifically provide for payment of preferred creditors in priority over unsecured creditors.

Directors

- Stay of proceedings activated
- Proposal can release directors
- Court can indemnify directors, grant a charge, and/or remove directors

Proposal Trustee

- Similar to a monitor
- Oversees restructuring process, liaises with all parties
- Administers distributions

10. RESTRUCTURING

(5) BIA Proposals — Real Property Leases

Special rules for disclaiming real property leases include a need for 30 days' notice of disclaimer to property owner, and the owner has 15 days to dispute the disclaimer. The debtor must show that it would not be able to make a proposal without the disclaimer.

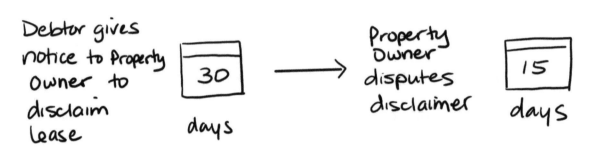

- The property owner has no claim for accelerated rent (unlike the CCAA).
- The debtor elects in the proposal whether the property owner will file proof of claim or base it on a formula.
- The formula is the lesser of rent for one year + 15 percent of the remainder of the term or 3 years' rent.

10. RESTRUCTURING

(5) BIA Proposals — Other Areas

• Executory Contracts

Functions the same as under the CCAA; however, unlike the CCAA in order to disclaim an executory contract, the individual must be carrying on a business and the contract must be related to the business. The assignment of contracts also functions the same as under the CCAA with the exception of leases.

- Interim Sale of Assets
- Interim Financing
- Administration Charge

All function like they do under the CCAA.

10. RESTRUCTURING

(5) BIA Proposal – Claims

Crown Claims

As in bankruptcy, statutory deemed trusts in favour of the Crown are not effective except for source deductions. The Crown is not a secured creditor with respect to source deductions for voting. The court cannot approve of a proposal unless it provides for payment of source deductions.

Wage & Pension Claims

Wage and pension protection does not apply, but a court cannot approve a proposal unless it provides for payment of wage and contribution arrears.

Equity Claims

As with the CCAA, equity claims cannot be provided for in the proposal unless all non-equity claims are paid in full first.

10. RESTRUCTURING

(5) BIA Proposals — Process Failures: Creditor Attacks

Creditors can cause a proposal to fail before a vote by making a motion to have the proposal deemed refused. Reasons for refusal:

  a) debtor not acting in good faith,

  b) proposal will likely not be accepted, or

  c) there is material prejudice to the creditors.

Creditors can also terminate a stay and/or oppose the extension of a stay, causing the proposal to fail.

10. RESTRUCTURING

(5) BIA Proposals — Process Failures: Deemed Assignments

There are various different situations where the proposal process can fail, resulting in a deemed assignment in bankruptcy. This can occur in the following scenarios:

- deemed refusal
- failure to file proposal
- negative creditor vote
- failure to file cash flow
- termination of a stay
- court does not approve
- proposal annulment for non-performance

10. RESTRUCTURING

CCAA and BIA Proposal Differences

Under BIA proposals (unlike CCAA proposals):

- There is no monetary threshold.

- There is an automatic 30-day stay of proceedings with an 180-day limit.

- A BIA proposal can be flipped into a CCAA proceeding but not vice versa.

- There is no critical supplier provision.

- Bankruptcy is automatic if the unsecured creditors vote no to the proposal.

- Differences in the claims process and requirements to pay preferred claims.

- Differences in the treatment of real property lease disclaimers.

- Differences in annulments and deemed assignment on breach.

11. INTERNATIONAL INSOLVENCIES

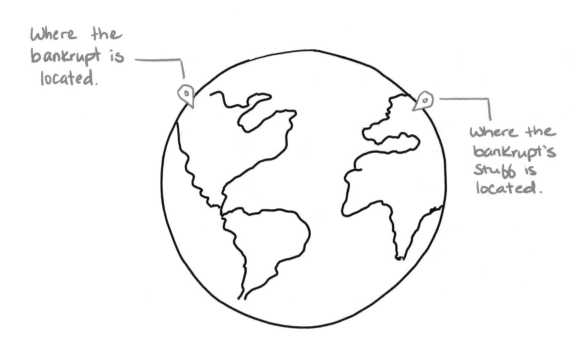

Where the bankrupt is located.

Where the bankrupt's stuff is located.

11. INTERNATIONAL INSOLVENCIES

In an increasingly global economy, there are millions of businesses with multiple operations in various international jurisdictions. While Canadian laws may state that they apply anywhere in the world, in reality, a foreign jurisdiction must recognize the Canadian law in order for it to apply in the foreign jurisdiction. For example:

A Canadian trustee cannot seize a Canadian bankrupt's property located inside the United States based on the BIA or a Canadian court order unless authorized by a US court.

11. INTERNATIONAL INSOLVENCIES

Comity

Comity is when one country recognizes the legislative, executive, or judicial acts of another country. Based on comity, Canadian courts can enforce foreign orders where there is a "substantial connection" between the foreign jurisdiction and the defendant.

But based on the principle of comity, this order is enforceable in the United States!

Usually comity is based on the centre of main interest, such as the debtor's registered office, their headquarters, or where command/control resides.

11. INTERNATIONAL INSOLVENCIES

International Treaties

International treaties between countries are what help to formalize recognition and promote greater cooperation when it comes to insolvency proceedings. Europe has the European Insolvency Regulation and the United Nations has the UN Commission on International Trade Law (UNCITRAL).

Canada and the United States have both adopted a modified version of the UNCITRAL.

11. INTERNATIONAL INSOLVENCIES

Cross-Border Insolvencies

In 2009, the BIA and CCAA were amended to adopt the UNCITRAL Model Law (with some variations), which deals with foreign reorganizations. A full and complete hearing is known as a **plenary** proceeding. A secondary/complementary proceeding is an **ancillary** proceeding. Cross-border insolvency legislation is meant to foster cooperation, provide legal certainty, and administrative efficiency, maximize debtor's property value, and rescue troubled businesses.

11. INTERNATIONAL INSOLVENCIES

CCAA Part IV Foreign Reorganizations

CCAA Part IV, dealing with foreign reorgs, makes a distinction:

foreign main proceedings vs foreign non-main proceedings.

↓   ↓

- A foreign proceeding in a jurisdiction where the debtor has the centre of its main interests.
- Absent proof to contrary, it will be debtor's registered office.

- A foreign proceeding other than a foreign main proceeding.

A foreign proceeding means:

- outside of Canada
- deals with collective creditor's interests
- subject to supervision of foreign court

A foreign representative means:

- person authorized in foreign proceeding to monitor debtor or act as representative

11. INTERNATIONAL INSOLVENCIES

Foreign Main Proceeding — Automatic Relief

CCAA provides for automatic relief on making an order to recognize a foreign main proceeding, including:

1) ordering a stay or any period the court deems necessary on all proceedings against the debtor,

2) restraining further proceedings,

3) prohibiting commencement of other actions, and

4) prohibiting the debtor company from disposing of property outside the normal course of business (in Canada).

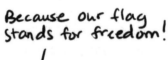

11. INTERNATIONAL INSOLVENCIES

Foreign Main Proceeding — Supplementary Relief

The court also has wide discretion to grant supplementary relief that can be applied even to foreign non-main proceedings where no automatic relief has been granted.

(!) Note: Recognizing the proceeding does not mean that the orders are automatically given full force and effect. Orders must each be recognized and given force individually.

11. INTERNATIONAL INSOLVENCIES

Final Points on Foreign Reorgs

After a foreign order is recognized, an appointment of an information officer (similar to a monitor) is made, a stay of proceeding is ordered, an administration charge is placed, and arrangements are made for interim financing.

(!) Note: The court can still refuse to make orders that are contrary to public policy.

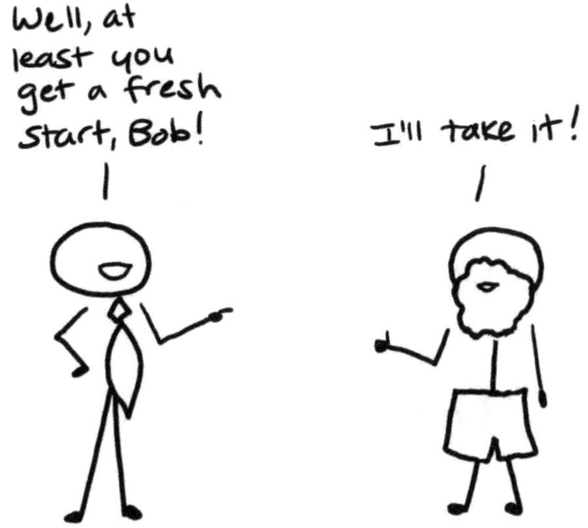

-the end-

—ABOUT THE AUTHOR—

Wela is a proud Albertan living in New York City. A former corporate lawyer in Toronto and in New York City, she now spends her time running a Brooklyn based ed-tech start-up and writing visual legal guides. On the off chance you catch her not working, she can be spotted stuffing her face, usually with potatoes. See what she's up to at **www.nybarpicturebook.com**

—OTHER BOOKS—

- NEW YORK BAR PICTURE BOOK
- CONTRACTS LAW PICTURE BOOK